First Edition: 2013

Printed in Beirut

P. O. Box: 50313 Jeddah 21523
Phone: (02) 6827968 _ (02) 6827701
Fax: (02) 6916473
Email: dar_alramak@hotmail.co.uk
abufarah58@hotmail.com

Book designed by: Salma Ghulman
Email: salma.ghulman@gmail.com

PROVEN BILLIONAIRES' FORMULA

Adula AlBakheel

ALL THE BOOKS YOU WILL NEVER HAVE THE TIME TO READ - IN ONE

CAUTION: THIS BOOK HAS THE RECIPE OF SUCCESS

YOU
WON.

DEDICATION

I would like to dedicate this book to the child you once were – when you believed everything was possible and nothing was out of reach; may this book be a leading factor in that child's rebirth. I would also like to dedicate it to every failure, hardship, and adversity surrounding you right now. Why? Because you picked up this book - **YOU WON.**

.

WHAT IS THIS BOOK ABOUT AND WHO IS IT FOR?

Simply stated, this book has the findings of over 300 business and psychology books merging into one all-you-need-to-know-about-success book and it is for people who want to prove they are destined for greatness – because we all are.

After coming across every type of business, psychology, and success book, I compiled the rational and irrational, the feasible and infeasible, and the sane and insane ideas together in this easy-read simple book.

Now, here's a proper introduction

They say a journey of a thousand miles starts with a single step; or 2500 Wal-Mart stores start with one tiny store in Arkansas. The important question is: **what happened before that single step or tiny store?**

Studying thousands of success stories of different individuals in different fields, I have come to find that the steps leading up to the journey are as following:

Step 1	It starts with an idea – an idea to take that journey.
Step 2	It builds up with an evaluation of the idea – determining the feasibility of embarking on that journey.
Step 3	It moves onto reality when it is declared – declaration of the journey.
Step 4	Time is managed in a way that fulfills utmost dedication to the journey.
Step 5	Understanding how to keep one eye at the journey and the other eye at bigger opportunities expedites the entire process and brings along greater opportunities.
Step 6	By step 6, a person's enthusiasm is truly at test. Exhibiting unwavering enthusiasm towards the same journey shows that it is a calling
Step 7	A detailed, long-term plan that explains how one will reach to one's desired destination is comprised and prepared for.
Step 8	Once everything is prepared for and ready, one's tendency to procrastinate skyrockets. Overcoming that tendency to procrastinate and taking the first step is what will determine the rest of your career.
Step 9	As every journey, a bumpy road is bound to be stumbled upon. If a person has the enthusiasm of step 6 and the dedication of step 4, no bump can defer the process of reaching your destination.
Step 10	The tenth step is to understand that going to the top is easier than staying there. Successful people of the 10 steps understand that every opportunity is waiting to be seized and just because they have seized one, does not mean they have to stop there.

Success is an amazing journey that is reached by seizing life's golden opportunities, and to further explain that fact, just look at all of those self-made billionaires and millionaires and tell me what did they have when they were first starting out that you don't?

There are 1210 billionaires in the world as of March 2011, and let's say 50 percent of them were fortunate enough to inherit the money, what about the other 50 percent?
People make excuses and justifications about the rich – like how they got the money through luck or how they never had to work a day in their lives, what they should really justify or explain is: why are you giving them excuses when you can start on eliminating yours?

Life is not supposed to be such a difficult jouney, and the reason it has become such a difficult jouney to some is because some people's mindsets are completely frozen in the generation in which they were raised in. As time goes by, things tend to change, and as more time goes by, everything tends to change. The world is becoming dominated by techonlogy and some people here today are still stuck in light bulb amazement. Well, yes we do have light bulbs now and candles are only used for ornamental (AKA, romantic) purposes, but there's more where that came from.

The world is there, you might as well try it out and this book will show you how to put it to the test and win. The chapters of this book are the requirements of success, and they are as follows:

Each and every one of these elements is extremely important for success, and as I mentioned: many people find excuses without the mere consideration of trying. If the world continued implementing this form of behavior, then this generation will not progress; families will complain about the lack of money and how hard it is to get money until they implant these toxic thoughts into their children's mentality, these thoughts will be the face of action thereafter. In this book, you'll read the words "passion", "tenacity" and "determination" a lot because they are the core ingredients to success.

Monetary Formula

"Money is not the root of all evil, the love of money is."

When you come to look at all the "special secrets" of the rich, you'll notice that there is no one special secret. There are, however, numerous small secrets that are equivalently important. You will also notice that in every element of their work, they will state, "without this or that, I wouldn't be where I am today" or "this is the key to the whole thing" which defines my point: the rich place a high importance to details – why? Because attention to detail defines a perfectionist. You just have to focus on all of the small tasks all at once and make it work.

The world is my yummy oyster and I choose to eat it. Fortunately, I was blessed to know what I want to do from a young age, but for those who have the words "it's too late" in their dictionary, (we'll get to the "it's too late" excuse in the coming chapters) then don't feel discouraged in anyway. Never ever put a barrier between your passion and your age, or your financial status, or any other excuse because it's in our control to obliterate these excuses if we desire to, and those who desire to do so are rewarded with happiness and financial abundance.

It's only human to have a keen interest in money; some people won't admit it, but that's reality. Had I not found my true passion, the thing that gets me on the edge of my seat and heart-rate up, I would have ventured on every career to find the passion that I'll choose to make my money provider, and here's how I would start:
I would take deep consideration and contemplation about each and every action I do in my daily life until I reach an action that requires payment, I stop and think of a way to conceive a creative way, unique approach to this money-providing task, I determine whether it suits me and whether I can see myself doing it better than anyone else, I provide it better than anyone else. I serve the people a better service, and people serve me financially.

That was a lot of talking, but let me exemplify:

When I am on my way rent an office to start my own business, I stop and ask myself: can I buy an office building and rent it to those who want an office? I have to determine whether I feel comfortable with it, then I analyze the reason to why the owners of office buildings already have one, and how they did it. So I delve into the commercial real estate industry to learn some more, once I have learnt enough and done my analysis on this industry, I apply for a mortgage that is best suitable for my conditions, look for a building, do an inspection, get an appraisal, and after I have acquired everything, I will get myself an office in *my* building (rent-free) and enjoy the extra money that tenants pay me. Knowing that the money that tenants pay me is what is going to pay the monthly payment of my mortgage, but the 'leftovers' are mine.

That sounds easy, doesn't it? Well, it mostly is. If you examine a field and determine that it is not comfortable for you, then it is simple: don't pursue it. You have to love it because it will require a lot of your effort and enjoyment.

Now it is true that one greatly pursued idea is much better than hundreds of brilliant ideas that are unpursued, thus, the belief in your idea, determination in your vision, and sharing it with others is what will compel you to go on and continue.

What if your passion has never been a career that someone has leaped on before? Even better! Why? Because working automobiles were extremely scarce, almost unheard of in the 1890's. Had anyone built a career out of it? Nope, did that fact discourage Henry Ford? Nope. In fact, at the age of sixteen, he was an apprentice for a mechanic – steadily advancing; he became chief engineer at the Edison Illuminating Company. Is chief engineer of a large company satisfactory for an average man? Yes. Was it satisfactory for Ford? No. Henry Ford devoted his free time in engineering and in building an automobile company while working for Thomas Edison's company. Had I been around in the day to see a determined and ambitious Henry Ford, I would've guessed that he'd make it. And he did.

"A WINDOW OF OPPORTUNITY WON'T OPEN ITSELF " Dave Weinbaum

I

CHAPTER ONE

Follow your passion and construct a goal

> *"Our ideals resemble the stars, which illuminate the night. No one will ever be able to touch them. But the men, who, like the sailors on the ocean, take them for guides, will undoubtedly reach their goal."*
>
> **Carl Schurz**

A few years ago, I thought people were meant to hate their jobs and burdenly anticipate tomorrow for yet another day of arduous work, and in reality that is what most children and teenagers think. Through observing billionaires, looking into biographies, and studying the psychology behind the middle-class workers and the richest 5% of the world, I was fortunate enough discover the concealed facts that very few see. All of those who dislike waking up in the morning and going to work are those who dislike what they are doing, and the best news is that it does not have to be you.

There are various fields that provide people the chance to do anything they want, why is it that most of the people choose the field they hate the most? Well there are 3 phases before that happens:

Phase #1 – Found a job that pays well for an inexperienced graduate.

Phase #2 – Maintain security and comfort.

Phase #3 – Unable to walk away and risk the security.

And here is how it should go:

Phase #1 – Choose a college major that truly captivates your interest.

Phase #2 – After graduation, you have two choices:

> A- Look for a temporary job that you might consider for the mere motive of the experience and then later work on reaching higher places and promotions.

> B- Start your own business in that field and do it better than anyone else.

Phase #3 – Be financially worry free doing what you love for a living instead of being financially unstable doing what you hate.

Passion is what motivates you to keep going, and goals are your map and guide to pursue that passion. You will not be fulfilled if you don't pursue that urging goal.

So, why am I blabbering on about determination and goals like a whiney child? Because your goal and your determination go hand in hand: after the goal comes, the determination will follow. A goal is a mental picture that you engrave in your mind, or an actual picture that you frame and put on your nightstand. It is stable, and it doesn't rise and fall.

Determination, while still of utmost importance, comes in number two because it's unstable. One day it is as high as mount Everest, the second it is wavering like a tsunami. Do not put yourself down if your determination wavers; it is very much ok for as long as you have the reason you need to remind you why you built this goal in the first place. Thus, once you have a clear goal, you'll reach it – whether your determination is high or low because you know what you want.

Every person is a genius in a specific field, the key to awakening this genius is to find that field in which your genius lies in. To find that field you have to determine which of these IQs you excel in:

Verbal/Linguistic Intelligence

To excel in reading, writing, speaking, and conversing.

Logical/Mathematical Intelligence

To excel in numbers and computing skills, to enjoy playing with numbers and puzzles, balancing everything out, evening every relationship out.

Visual/Spatial Intelligence

To excel in creating mental images, joining colors, creating graphical images.

Bodily/Kinesthetic Intelligence

To excel in physical coordination, expressing oneself physically, dancing, playing sports, conceiving solutions for complex problems.

Musical Intelligence

To have a musical ear, coming up with melodies and rhythmic words, singing, expressing oneself through music.

Interpersonal Intelligence

To excel in communicating and understanding other people.

Intrapersonal Intelligence

To excel in understanding your most inner thoughts and emotions; to have the ability to control them (to have their own little world).

Naturalistic Intelligence

To love nature and the environment, to love animals and plants.

No one knows you better than yourself (and if someone does know you better than you know yourself, ask for their kind assistance), so you must determine which kind of intelligence you strongly possess and work with it. Grow it and make it your money-provider because this way, you will be the best at it and once you're the best at it you will get to the top and get rewarded beautifully.

I wrote this book when I was sixteen years old and published it when I became twenty, since that time I have constructed an efficient and thorough plan to make a dream of mine a reality I live in.

My passion is real estate; building tall, unique buildings that will carry my name and will shape the city that I build in to be specific. Like a teenager filled with dopamine, head over heels in love, I get butterflies at the mere sight of skyscrapers. Whenever I see a picture or a video of a construction team working my heart starts racing and my mind flames up with ideas. I meticulously know my goal, and I also know the obstacles that I will be faced with.

It is important to be optimistic, however, it is equally as important to be realistic. Back to my point, I have found ways, by constructing my goal, to beat those obstacles. The biggest obstacle I faced was coming from a conservative cultural background that revolved around my norms, traditions, and hertiage. I do not want to waste your time talking about the obstacles I faced, but the point I want to raise you is this: I have worked myself around it and found a way to live independently because anyone can find excuses if they want to. I could have turned my back on any of my goals and went shopping like any other teenager but I have a dream, I have a passion and I am filled with the urge to fulfill it, and I will not rest until I do.

I have read over 300 business and psychology books and the one thing that all of them have in common is the significant role passion plays in successful people's lives. Passion is a primary reason for a lifetime worth of happiness and self-fulfillment.

Think about it, how could conquering the impossible be impossible if by breaking out the term itself, we will find it saying "I'm possible"? Conquering the impossible is not so impossible when the people and thoughts that surround you say that it is not impossible, and that is where caregivers or parents' role come in.

Our present attitudes are habits built from the feedback of our parents, friends, and society that forms both our self-image and our world-image.

Parents are the role models for their children; whatever they say has a huge impact on their children, whether they see it or not. Supportive and encouraging parents, in my opinion, are one of the greatest blessing anyone could ever have. So, please Mr. and Mrs. Parents, your children are the next generation and it is your duty to paint that generation beautifully.

The truth is that the main reason people do not get what they want is simply because they do not know what they want. The main reason people do not know what they want is because of the lack of experimentation, conviction, and direction. When individuals fail to experiment with their likes and dislikes – experimenting with a guitar, for example – they will not know what they are destined to be, nor will they know their true genius.

The late Steve Jobs, known for his incredible entrepreneurial skills, innovation, and creativity in Apple Company, followed this theory in innovating new products for the company – and I quote him: "People don't know what they want until you show it to them."
This same indecisive quality is what drives consumer behaviors and impulsive spending in the markets: people do not know what they want.

"But it is too late to start now"

This is the most common excuse I have heard until now. And whenever I stumble upon that excuse, I go tracing back to the story of Colonel Sanders, the founder of KFC, the fast-food chain.
Colonel Sanders was born in Henryville, Indiana. His father died when he was five years old and since his mother worked, he was required to cook for his family. He dropped out of school in the seventh grade. During his teenage years, Sanders held many jobs including firefighter, steamboat driver, insurance salesman, railroad worker, farmer, and he also enlisted in the Army as a private in 1907 in Cuba.
At the age of 40, Sanders cooked chicken dishes for people who stopped at his service station in Corbin, Kentucky. Since he did not have a restaurant, he served customers in his living quarters in the service station. Eventually, his local popularity grew, and Sanders moved to a motel and restaurant that seated 142 people and worked as the chef.

This inspirational story about this man is not a one-in-a-million type of situation, Colonel's company was founded when he was 62 years old and his company is now in charge of over 750,000 employees, so don't use the phrase nor the excuse "but it's just too late" because it is never too late and now you have Colonel's to prove that.

Make your passion your money provider.

Side notes   The percentage of students with an undecided major is 10% and the percentage of college students switching their majors before graduating is 44% (Source: National Center for Edutation Statistics). I do not believe that undecided majors show a lack of determination or motive, they might even have double the motive that decided majors have. However, I do believe that high school freshmen should have the luxury of test-driving majors just like brand new cars. We buy cars, use them, and either sell them later on or just leave them to deteriorate. Keep in mind that cars are not a life-long decisions, nor do they contribute nor determine who you are. College majors and education fields define who you are, and test-driving careers should be a must for every high-school student.

Sit down and specify the likely date you want to retire by. I have set this date since I was fifteen years old and because of that date I have a clear vision that is driven by a meticulously written plan that supports my date.

II

CHAPTER TWO

Believe in Yourself

"Whether you believe you can or you can't, you're right"
Henry Ford
"You are today where your thoughts have brought you; you will be tomorrow where your thoughts take you."
James Allen

I have seen hundreds of books in every bookstore, library, and online websites talking about the phenomena of emotional intelligence; after a while I came to a conclusion:

They are not exaggerating.

Emotions and imagination have a profound effect on every single thing we do, whether it was in our daily lives or business, we should probably give it more credit than what we are giving it right now and learn how to use it to our advantage because it could be a huge asset or a huge liability; it all depends on how you choose to use it.

One of the primary reasons that millionaires and billionaires exist is because they never underestimate themselves; they simply have a dream and a focus that is so ingrained in themselves that the only option is achieving it.

The only limitations that exist are those that we place amongst ourselves.

A couple of months ago, I was speaking with a man that works as a personal driver in Saudi Arabia. He was talking to me about money, and he said "I had a lot of opportunities growing up, and if I took them I would have had an apartment in a building like this!" then he pointed at a stingy, old and almost abandoned apartment building that was at least fifty years old. Then I realized, he was confining himself to that kind of dream where this hideous apartment building was as good as it gets. And too bad, because that is as good as it will get for him.

Limiting yourself to one standard of the luxuries in this world should be a crime. Cutting out luxuries that make you happy from your daily life to be a millionaire in the long-term is, with all due respect, ludicrous. Why be rich in the long-term when the world is screaming with opportunities that you can seize to be rich in the short-term? An example of this would be people who choose not to buy from Starbucks because of their four-dollar-a-latte prices and instead go buy a $3 latte to put the extra $1 in their retirement fund. NO! Living life with such limited measures and such suffocating spending habits is an impairment to the name of life. Now, I am not saying that spending twenty dollars a day on coffee means you have made it; I am saying that this let-me-save-one-dollar-and-deprive-myself-of-the-green-beautiful-lady-symbol-in-my-coffee-cup mentality will never put you on the road to riches. It will only put you on the road to retiremental financial comfort – and if that is all you want, then this book is not for you. This book is for people who want to buy a Maserati just because they accidentally passed by the showroom on their way to their golf court.

Saving every penny for retirement or for a vacation home is not my definition of rich, and it should not be yours. While I do agree with the idea of leaving a sum of your money untouched, I disagree with the idea of preventing yourself from basic spending rituals just to enjoy your money later on. This is where this book might provide a controversial aspect or two in financial beliefs and stereotypes.

What Donald Trump, Richard Branson, Warren Buffett, and many other billionaires have in common is simple: they think BIG. By thinking big, I mean instead of thinking in terms of thousands, they chose to think in term of billions; instead of aspiring to build a multi-million dollar company, they decided to change their dreams with the change of one word, multi-billion.

In doing the math, we find that starting big means that if you lose, you will lose big; that is not particularly true. Starting a business requires two things: funding and time. If you have one of these, or if you are willing to contribute one of these, you are half way there. Since most people only have time or funding, the best solution to getting both is through networking. How? By starting something with someone who has what you lack. People who do not have the funding, usually will make the time; and people who do have the funding usually do not have the time. Joining a partnership, starting a big project and owning a percentage is one of the fastest ways to get your hands on some money.

Donald Trump and Robert Kiyosaki stated an amazing theory that I think everyone should apply, which is: why live below your means when you can live up to it?

Excuses:

I know for a fact that if the required determination existed, all excuses will vanish; and if, however, the lack of determination existed then all you will ever accomplish is going to be excuses.

Remember when all you wanted for dinner were cookies or candy, and your caregiver wouldn't allow it? Why couldn't you find excuses not to eat those cookies and candy then? Because you desperately wanted them! If you didn't desperately want them you would find that there were many excuses not to eat them, i.e. my stomach would hurt!

Side notes   We were all born a blank-slate, even if the never-ending debate between nature against nurture persists, we can all agree that nurture contributes drastically to who we grow up to be. Prior to the taking place of nurture, when we were mere infants, we knew nothing about anything; nonetheless, people were born to improvise and learn on most of the aspects they wanted to mature in. The reason I speak about tabula rasa (another reference to a blank slate) is because I want to emphasize the fact that at some point, billionaires knew nothing about their field of business. So, now is the time to think of the infamous question, "why them and not me?" and to realize that while some billionaires may have been born to financial abundance, others started with less than what you have right now. In other words, you do not have an excuse so stop looking for excuses and take action.

THE POWER OF IMAGINATION

"There are no rules of architecture for a castle in the clouds."
G.K. Chesterton

Being a guitarist, I have witnessed so many sleepless nights where I would stay twisting and turning in bed imagining every part of a gig I would have the next day and exactly how I would play my guitar. After hours of unsuccessful sleeping attempts, I would go to my family's living room and find my brother sitting; and when he would ask me why I did not sleep, the only answer that made sense to me was, "I am busy with my imagination." But I did not want to sound like a nutcase, so I would just tell him I am hungry. By the time I would finish imagining every detail of the gig, I would finally doze off. Next day comes, and I am in the middle of my performance only to realize that every detail I imagined last night was actually happening.

The reason I am using a personal reference to this chapter is because I have personally tested the power of visualization and imagination countless times only to find that my imagination becomes reality – and the more detailed the imaginative picture is, the better.

Wikipedia.com's definition:

Imagination is the ability to form mental images. It helps provide meaning to experience and understanding to knowledge; it is a fundamental facility through which people make sense of the world, and it also plays a key role in the learning process. A basic training for imagination is the listening to storytelling (narrative), in which the exactness of the chosen words is the fundamental factor to 'evoke worlds'.

It is accepted as the innate ability and process to invent partial or complete personal realms within the mind from elements derived from sense perceptions of the shared world.

"A fundamental facility through which people make sense of the world." I would like to repeat that sentence 10 times, but for the sake of not making this sound like a recitation class, I won't.

The first step to attaining something is by imagining it. Imagine it with precise detail, most importantly, imagine it positively.

One of the most wonderful documentaries that briefly mentions the power of imagination and visualization is The Secret which is based on the best-selling book, "The Secret" by Rhonda Byrne. I will quote this story from the book itself:

"Knowing the law of attraction, I wanted to really put it to use and to see what would happen. In 1995 I started to create something called a Vision Board, where I take something that I want to achieve, or something that I want to attract, like a car or a watch or the soul mate of my dreams, and I put a picture of what I want up on this board. Every day I would sit in my office and I would look up at this board and I would start to visualize. I would really get into the state of having already acquired it.

I was getting ready to move. We put all the furniture, all the boxes, into storage, and I made three different moves over a period of five years. And then I ended up in California and bought this house, renovated it for a year, and then had all the stuff brought from my farmer home five years earlier. One morning my son Keenan came into my office, and one of the boxes that was sealed for five years was right at the doorstep. He asked, "What's in the boxes, Daddy?" And I said, "Those are my Vision Boards." He then asked, "What's a Vision Board?" I said, "Well, it's where I put altlmy goals up. I cut them out and I put all my goals up as something that I want to achieve in my life." Of course at five and a half years old he didn't understand, and so I said, "Sweetheart, let me just show you, that'll be the easiest way to do it."

I cut the box open, and on one Vision Board was a picture of a home that I was visualizing five years earlier. What was shocking was that we were living in that house. Not a house like it—I actually bought my dream home, renovated it, and didn't even know it. I looked at that house and I started to cry, because I was just blown away. Keenan asked, "Why are you crying?" "I finally understand how the law of attraction works. I finally understand the power of visualization. I finally understand everything that I've read, everything that I've worked with my whole life, the way I've built companies. It worked for my home as well, and I bought our dream home and didn't even know it."

Have a goal, write it down, put it in a place where you will always see it, read it aloud twice a day, and your subconscious mind will take care of the rest.

Actions are forms of energy that are possessed by the power of thoughts and imagination. Knowing this, work on using it for your advantage. You become what you think of, and what you think of is basically your imagination.

Never underestimate yourself or the power of imagination and never confine yourself to what you think you can achieve, confine yourself to- that's where I am stuck. So confine yourself to: NOTHING. Have no limitations, believe in the power of humanity and the powerful forces we possess.

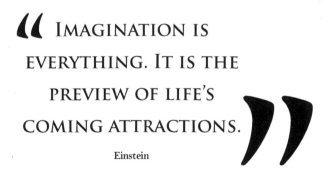

❝ IMAGINATION IS EVERYTHING. IT IS THE PREVIEW OF LIFE'S COMING ATTRACTIONS. ❞

Einstein

THE POWER OF POSITIVE THINKING

"Most folks are about as happy as they make up their minds to be."
Abraham Lincoln

Everyone was going on and on about the power of positive thinking until eventually I came through a book that changed my pattern of thinking The Power of Positive Thinking by Norman Vincent Peale. Here are the basic points of positive thinking:

• Whatever utters from your mouth works its way through your mind. Whatever lingers in your mind will find a way to your actions.
• Whenever a negative thought arises, delete it with a positive one.
• Avoid the presence of negative people; they are toxins that will find a way into your system and before you know it, you will be negative yourself.
• Expect the best and you will get the best.
• Stick to your beliefs and respect them. You will amount to whatever you believe in.
• Surround yourself with people who think positively.
• Anger and worry are both destructive emotions, and we hold the power to reduce them to the minimum extent.

All of us get caught up in strenuous phases of our lives from time to time; such challenging phases provide us with the ideal way of learning. As Confucius said, "I hear and I forget. I see and I remember. I do and I understand." It is by experience that we grow, and it is also by contentment that we become fulfilled in being avid believers that the reason for every difficulty is because a good day got caught up in traffic. Trust me, there is a reason for everything in our lives, and it is up to you to decide whether these reasons are for your own good or not.

I can go on and on, but these factors are the rudimentary of positive thinking and if we can attain them, this world would be much, much easier.

Praise yourself and others. Dream of success until you live that dream. If you can dream it, you can live it.

Self-rights:

Kindness and reverence shouldn't only be applied to others, but to ourselves as well. Self-respect is why we owe it to ourselves to at least give the opportunities around us a chance to be seized.

Working a hundred hours a week on a job you dislike is treating yourself unjust. Why allow yourself to be jaded and fray and use every useful force that you have on something that you don't even enjoy for the sake of someone else (your employer) to get rich? Look through the arena, expand your field of vision and do something that you won't resent waking up to do. Remember: if you don't work on building your dreams, someone else will hire you to work on theirs.

Reward Yourself:

It is known that success brings with it it's various rewards, but some people tend to be cheap and too frugal that they are still living below their means.

Ingvar Feodor Kamprad, the Swedish entrepreneur, who founded IKEA is the richest person in Europe with a total net worth of $42.2 billion. That amount of money would be sufficient to last him if he chose to spend $1 million a day for the rest of his life. However, you will be surprised to know that he takes the subway to work, and he drives an old Volvo.

Now I agree on the idea of spending money wisely, but there's a thin line between wise and cheap.

Enter a business expecting to win, and you will get those results. The world agrees with whatever you expect from it, **expect the best and you will get the best.**

III

CHAPTER THREE

WRITE IT DOWN

"A plan unwritten is not a plan at all."

You never know when you might need a pen or a small notebook, and it is very hard to keep track of every important note you have written, but the good news is that in this generation dominated by technology there are upgraded and easier programs and methods to noting down whatever you have in mind.

Average workers give 25% of their efforts to what they do, so it is inevitable for people to be amazed by those who work with 50% of their efforts, not to mention those who work with the outstanding 100% of their efforts. One of the reasons those who put in a 100% in working do so is because they have all of their belongings intact; whenever they want something they know exactly where it is and thus they do not waste time trying to find it.

I have said earlier how, when each individual writes their goal down and puts it where they can see it and read it aloud everyday, it presents a psychological impact on this individual and that is why it is so important, once again: never underestimate the little things you do that get restored in your subconscious brain and implement action.

How to Write your Goal?

Write your goal in a positive way

Your subconscious mind will carry it as a tool and turn it into reality, the more positive instructions you give it, the more positive results you will get.

Write your goals in complete detail

If you want to be rich, you have to determine how much money you want. Saying "plenty of money" is not meticulous enough to make it. Don't say, "I want a house" say "I want X square feet, 2 bathrooms, etc."

Write in present tense

Your subconscious mind is smart enough to distinguish the difference between present tense and past tense.

Writing down your dreams is also one of the first steps to achieving them because it helps you visualize your goals. You'll be filled with the feeling of declaring this visible goal not only to yourself, but to the world as well. It is a valuable tool for applying those dreams into your life.

There is a connection between your pen and your brain, use it for your benefit and learn how to make it work for you, because it can!

Your office and workspace present a portrait of your life, it is either organized (which means that your brain and thoughts are organized and prioritized), or unorganized (which means distortion in thoughts and in priorities).

IV

CHAPTER FOUR

FOCUS AND DEDICATE ALL YOUR ENERGY INTO IT

"If I wanted to reach the goal I set for myself, I had to get at it and stay at it everyday. I had to think about it all the time."
Sam Walton
"Dedication involves making the space to let young ideas take hold; every tree was once a seed and every company was once an idea."
Zephyr Bloch-Jorgensen.

Let's start this chapter with stating the difference between knowing and doing. In order to move forward you must know and do. You won't go anywhere when you know and don't do, and you also won't go anywhere when you do and don't know; so know and do. Sorry for the headache.

Now let's continue this chapter with this inspiring story:

Donald J. Trump, the real estate developer was on the top of the world from 1974-1985. All of the deals he was putting together were on his side, and everything was going just as planned; until the feeling of ease eluded Trump and he felt it was ok to take his eyes away from the ball. In 1985-1990, his momentum decreased and he found himself in a continuous battle with the banks, with an enormous amount of money (billions) in loans. Why is it that a competent real estate investor sinks to billions of dollars in debt? It is all due to the lack of focus and momentum.

I define momentum as the speed of the chase, which is the demanding thrill of the moment. Once you lose that, you lost the grip you have on yourself. Focus is also the reason behind the ability to make fast decisions, which is important for the productivity of your every day.

There is a time for every successful business person to have so much going on, so many deals to close all at one certain time. Most people usually wonder how anyone can maintain his or her focus; there are three answers to that:

Answer #1

Being organized - as discussed in chapter 3.

Answer #2

Working 100% or applying the 80/20 rule - which we will discuss later.

Answer #3

Dedication - which we will discuss in this chapter.

Once you have instilled this business or goal of yours to the air you breathe, you will be an expert in the game and you will find it easy to make fast, good decisions.

Never accept any less than the total concentration and the total best from yourself on any small or big task.

Concentrate and focus greatly, when you work. Give a 100% or don't work at all.

Never do less than your utmost best, even if you were out of a job, be the best at being out of a job. Truth is, hard work pays off with interest, sometimes it pays off in the short-term, and sometimes it disguises in a long-term investment; have patience and see the results.

Self-Discipline

The famous Michelangelo di Lodovico Buonarroti Simoni, commonly known as MichelAngelo, was an Italian painter, architect, sculptor, poet, engineer, and the best-documented artist of the 16th century. Known for many of his outstanding and unrivaled work – David, the Sistine Chapel ceiling, the Pietà – he was a man with profound and determined discipline. In 1505 MichelAngelo was invited to Rome by Pope Julius II to build the Pope's tomb the statue of Mosses. MichelAngelo faced some interruption while he worked but he continued to work on the tomb for 40 years, it was left unfinished.

The major interruption for MichelAngelo was painting the Sistine Chapel, which took 4 years to complete; the composition contained a total of 300 figures and nine scenes including the Creation of Adam, Adam and Eve. MichelAngelo believed every stone had a sculpture within (the power of imagination).

Now if MichelAngelo was not filled with the combination of discipline and focus, would he of still been known after more than 500 years? His passion was painting and sculpturing, and he dedicated his life to his passion and was determined to be the best in his chosen field, and he succeeded.

He spent 40 years on a single sculpture - the Tomb. Imagine the discipline and persistence it takes to work on one project for forty consecutive years, and the fulfillment that comes after finishing it. Why can't we spend that much time on one thing that we want to do?

For the slightest example, when someone wants to bake a cake that tastes like the cake of a certain bakery, they spend no more than one week trying recipes until they give up. Now I am not saying spend 40 years on a cake, but why give up? Why not continue to pursue it until you make it? And if you really want to, you will.

The most common undisciplined case in today's generation is losing weight. The number one cause of obesity today is the lack of self-discipline. People tend to favor temporary gains over permanent favors, even though there is a profuse desire to lose weight, but there is no discipline.

Everyone has a passion that is worth fulfilling, it does not have to be painting nor sculpturing, but it can be achieved in the profound results that MichelAngelo achieved in painting and sculpturing as long as we exhibit an unwavering focus and discipline.

Success is a combination of desire, focus and persistence.

The first pillar to self-disciple is acceptance. Acknowledge the reality you chose upon yourself and fathom the fact that you are the only person with the power to change it. Retain the area in which you lack the required discipline and improve it, don't procrastinate on improving those areas for when you need them.

DEDICATION

Being dedicated to something means setting your pupose on a clear vision that is focused on a bigger pictureand aimed towards the light you see at the end of the tunnel. Disregard the discomfort along the bumpy road. If you know exactly where you want to be in twenty years, you will find a way to get there. However, if you do not have a clear vision, you will burn fuel without reaching anywhere. What I mean by dedication is to be passionate enough about something that devoting your entire energy to it feels like a piece of cake.

Dedication and commitment are key aspects to success in your desired field, because when you're truly dedicated and truly committed you will excel and be the best in that field, not only will it affect you in a positive way emotionally, but it will also affect you in a positive way financially.

You must make your goal the air you breathe; surround yourself with the beauty of achieving it, make it the focal point of where you stand, and syndicate every aspect of your life to it.

Side notes   The difference between winners and losers is that losers focus their thoughts and ideas on what they don't want in life whereas winners focus on what they do want.

Winners know when to quit and when to walk away, whereas losers are encumbered with an ego that suffocates them. Losers do not know when to quit; they cling to a failed idea to satisfy their egos.

Don't live with the Flintstones

"To succeed in this world, you have to change all the time"
Sam Walton

It is known that the only thing permanent in this world is the relevance of change. Successful companies succeed because of their virtue of being adaptable. Sticking to the methods that used to work fifty years ago is like an education system sticking to the same historical curriculum for generations.

A good example to this would be turning apartment buildings into condominiums. This was mostly common ten years ago until there became a surplus of condominiums and now turning apartment buildings into condominiums is no longer a profitable strategy. Now the profitable flip would be turning apartment buildings into hotels; and in another ten years, this would pass and a new strategy would be profitable.

Now those people that I am talking about (the non-rich) are those who are still transforming the apartment buildings into condominiums and wondering why they're not profiting from their investments.

V

CHAPTER FIVE

Use emotional intelligence for your benefit

"Let's not forget that the little emotions are the great captains of our lives and we obey them without realizing it."
Vincent Van Gogh.

In a 1994 report on the current state of emotional literacy, author Daniel Goleman stated:

"In navigating our lives, it is our fears and envies, our rages and depressions, our worries and anxieties that steer us day to day. Even the most academically brilliant among us are vulnerable to being undone by unruly emotions. The price we pay for emotional literacy is in failed marriages and troubled families, in stunted social and work lives, in deteriorating physical health and mental anguish and, as a society, in tragedies such as killings..."

Emotional intelligence is the ability to control one's emotions, and to act instead of react; emotional intelligence rescues you from precarious repent and regret. The root of the word "emotion" came from a Latin word which means "to move" and from the root of the word we can expand onto its true meaning; if we manage to control our emotions, we manage to direct (move) our future to where we set our minds on.

What wanders through your mind throughout your day is what will turn into what you do; the smallest and most minor thoughts you store in your mind get stuck in there and thereafter affect all of your future decisions.

Pessimism comes with a price; optimism comes with a reward.

What is Emotional Intelligence, really?

1. Self-awareness: acknowledging your feelings and perceiving them in a realistic way.

2.Mood management: knowing how to use the voice within to either brighten your mood or ravage it.

3.Self-motivation: assembling all of your emotions to the direction that leads you to the fulfillment of your goals, regardless of the self-doubt and fears that stand in your way.

4.Empathy: providing solace for others who feel hurt while commiserating for their behalf; having the ability to comfort them while putting yourself in their position.

5.Managing relationships: the ability to handle personal interactions with a rational response.

Physical vs. Emotional Intelligence

There's an inexplicable correlation between your physical state and your emotional state.

Every major or minor effort you take to improve your physical fitness will surge your self-esteem and enhance your social intelligence, leading to an improvement in the way you speak, act, and look. This will exude the charismatic quality that will make you speak with confidence and passion and will gain you the confidence and passion of others. Look the part, and you will become the part.

Training Emotional Intelligence

There are many ways to assess and handle emotional intelligence when you are angry: lay down, it is very difficult to stay angry when you lay down and/or count to ten or a hundred if you were really angry. It stimulates your ominous thoughts into actions of rationality.

These are two of the techniques that will help you cool down. Both anger and worry are destructive emotions, for starters don't congregate with a group of people who tend to worry or talk about the act of worrying. Emotions are contagious so be careful who you spend your time with.

Be careful what you agree upon and how you verbalize it. For example: when you say, "I am not going to smoke anymore" it is a good step, but the problem is that your subconscious mind will place an emphasis on the negative word, "not." Whereas when you say, "from today I am an ex-smoker" your subconscious mind will put that fact to reality.

Medical patients need emotional intelligence to heal, this story proves it: A guy was slightly sick and feeling delirious, he was not frail nor withered, it was a mere mild illness, but he kept screaming "I am going to die! I am going to die!" until his family called the paramedics, when they arrived they found him dead, his family asked for the cause of his demise. "It was emotional suicide" the paramedics said.

Note the difference between Believing in Yourself – knowing that you can do it – and Emotional Intelligence – using your emotions to help you do it, and using your emotions to be a better person.

**Control even the slightest negative emotions
and/or thoughts, and let a positive one conquer it.**

Side notes   Your thoughts are your reality; so we can conclude that it is not money that makes you rich, it is your ability to expand your reality.

VI

CHAPTER SIX

SIMULATE ENTHUSIASM

"Enthusiasm is the yeast that makes your hopes shine to the stars. Enthusiasm is the sparkle in your eyes, the swing in your gait. The grip of your hand, the irresistible surge of will and energy to execute your ideas."

Henry Ford

The word "enthusiasm" came from the Greek word, "enthousiasmos" which originally stood for inspiration or possession by a divine afflatus or by the presence of a God.

Enthusiasm is:

• A powerful force that gives us the strength to continue without the slightest doubt.

• An inclination that we should never give up until we accomplish what we were destined to achieve.

• A strong urge to never let a day pass without doing something towards your goal.

People say "enthusiasm is contagious," I can't defy that fact because it is true; notice how when you're listening to someone tell you about an incident that happened to him or her and when they are so enamored that they start talking very fast with hand signals and body movements, surely your reaction would be quite the same.

This fact is extremely important for speakers, they have to get enthusiastic and show it so that they will implement it to their audience. Notice any good, enthusiastic speaker and observe the audiences' reaction. They are most likely always sitting on the edge of their seats.

Enthusiasm & Communities

It is said, "Enthusiasm can be reflected & sustained by communities where it might die out in individuals." It is very common that the people who surround you might be negative or just want to bring you down with lame excuses such as "you can't do that" or "are you crazy? Even I couldn't do that" but it is very important to never let what other people say bring you down, it is essential to listen to opinions because you never know when an opinion might actually be beneficial to you, but don't let it affect your enthusiasm.

Enthusiasm vs. Passion

Enthusiasm relates to passion in so many ways and you can't have one without the other. Enthusiasm is bound to waver; keep in mind that enthusiasm is contagious, and if you find what you are enthusiastic about, you will find what you are passionate about. Follow both your enthusiasm ad passion and you will reach outstanding success

Side notes   We can compare ourselves to two classes of people: the less fortunate, and the fortunate. If we compare ourselves to the less fortunate, we will feel blessed and appreciative; if we compare ourselves to those who are more fortunate, we will feel encouraged to accomplish more so we can amount to them or we will feel bad about ourselves. The question is, what is the fine line between feeling both encouraged to accomplish and happy about our situation? Ask yourself this question, and come up with the answer that will help you excel whilst maintaining the positive, appreciative energy that will keep you going.

VII

CHAPTER SEVEN

Prepare, Prepare, Prepare

"Luck is a crossroad where preparation and opportunity meet"

What is preparation?
It is seizing the events of a situation before it happens.

You want to know why people make fortunes? It is because they form a thorough plan and stick to it. Billionaires and millionaires prepare for every single thing; they prepare before a meeting - by assessing expected questions and forming the appropriate answers so they won't get stuck. They prepare for a new deal - what they choose to do with it in both short-term and long-term. They prepare for dinner parties - forming conversation starters and ice breakers. They literally prepare for everthing.

Why prepare?
Many things can go wrong in whatever transaction we take, preparation puts you in a position that gives you leeway for when things go wrong, and better yet, it helps prevent such wrong happenings. Preparing always puts you one step ahead.

Preparation in Negotiation
People tend to negotiate every single day of their lives, even in the smaller happenings. It is said that the best negotiators are two year olds, and it is true; the reason to that is because they don't give up. They scream their heads off – and they won't give up until they get what they want.

We can all learn from two year olds, but if you don't have a two year old to learn from, then I'll tell you how:
• Know all you can about your negotiator.
• Know what your negotiator needs. Better yet, what he or she can't live without – talk to others who are involved in the deal and take their opinions on what they think your negotiator wants. Everything you know can be used as leverage.

- Knowledge is powerful - learn how to use it in the right timing and for the right motives.
- Be an easy person to deal with - be known for assembling deals not ravaging them.
- Be trust-worthy – in order for a negotiation to go well, people have to trust each other.
- Cool off the air - figure out something in common with your negotiator and talk about it to cool the air. Tension creates a vile vibe for negotiators, try to avoid that vibe.
- Find points where your negotiator is weak at and strengthen them in you.
- Evaluate, assess, and prepare – first of all, write down your objectives and what you hope to come out with when you finish the negotiation; second of all, write down expected questions regarding your and your negotiators objectives.
- Whatever quality it is that you are weak at, bring someone who has it and who is on your side in the negotiation with you – for example, if you are weak in numbers, bring someone who is good at them (your attorney, accountant, etc).
- Don't ever, ever show your negotiator your weak sides.

Preparation for the future

There's a book called Introducing NLP by Joseph O'Connor and John Seymour, which simplifies the preparation for your outcomes, and it goes like this:

Positive: think of what you want rather than what you don't want.

Own part: think of what you will actively do and what is within your control. Do not stress whatever is not within your control.

Specific: determine your desired outcome specifically and precisely.

Evidence: think of the sensory-based evidence that will let you know that you got what you want.

Resources: having adequate resources to achieve what you want.

Size: if the size of your outcome is big, then divide it into smaller outcomes and ask yourself "what prevents me from getting this?" if, however, the size of your outcome was small, then ask yourself "what will this minor outcome do for me?"

Ecology Frame: check the consequences in your life and relationships if you achieve your outcome, evaluate who this outcome will affect - other than yourself - and what will it do for your social life.

These are the preparations for your outcome. The final step, however, is taking action, which is the most important step. This step is easily achieved when you have the required determination.

Studying other subjects can help you in your business as long as you know how to correlate the information you have to your business and to your business skills, so here are non-business related books which I recommend to read in order to have your planning and futuristic plans intact:

- NLP & Relationships by Robin Prior and Joseph O'Connor.
- Emotional Intelligence by Daniel Goleman.
- The Power of Charm by Brian Tracey and Ron Arden.
- Don't be Sad by 'Aaidh ibn Abdullah al-Qarni.
- How to Talk to Anyone by Leil Lownders.

Billionaires and millionaires tend to create and prepare a plan and stick to it. Make it interesting and get the job done better than anyone.

VIII

CHAPTER EIGHT

SEE PROBLEMS AS
GOLDEN OPPORTUNITIES

"Opportunity is missed by most people because it is dressed in overalls and looks like work."
Henry Ford

Right now, I want you to imagine opportunities as a shy thirsty worker you can see from outside your glass window. He knows he needs to stand within his boundaries and keep on working without disturbing household members for a glass of water, unless someone in the house spotted him and opened the door to give the worker a glass of water. Now back to imagining opportunities as opportunities, they are within your reach if you only decide to be on the look out for them.

You can see opportunities through a window and in order to seize them you have to open the door. Few opportunities come knocking on your door without you inviting them in, it is in your ability to invite opportunities in and quench their thirst, because opportunities want to be seized.

Let me tell you a story once again about the real estate developer, Donald Trump.

After reading his autobiography, The Art of the Deal, Donald Trump started in real estate in 1974 in New York City, which at that time New York was facing a financial crisis, the vast majority saw it as the end for New York and was waiting for the city to declare bankruptcy; that was when Donald decided to seize this opportunity and place his entrepreneurial instincts to the test. He saw this financial crisis as the best opportunity and not only did he make the most of it, but he also enjoyed every minute of making the most of it. After evaluating the market, he knew that no city could replace New York City and realized that the financial crisis it was facing was anything but permanent. New York was bound for a recovery, and it was going to be a strong one.

One of the investments he made was buying the 40 Wall Street building for **$1 million**; he bought it knowing it requires a lot of work but it was all worth it because today it is worth over **$300 million!**

The world's best entrepreneurship program is in Babson College and they hold entrepreneurial forums every year where they gather the best entrepreneurs and speakers in the world to give a speech in this all-day forum. In 2011, the forum revolved around the question, "what is entrepreneurship, and why are entrepreneurs the richest people in the world?"

The answer that all of these famous influential speakers gave was this: entrepreneurs are business people that view problems as an opportunity to solve it – and idealistically, profit endlessly from it.

I could go on with this chapter giving you more examples of how current billionaires saw problems as disguised opportunities, but I am sure you got the gist by now.

Every minor or major event occurring in your life has a reason for happening. You might not discover that reason now, or in five years, or even in fifteen years but believe in the fact that you will eventually discover the reason why and it will be a good one.

How to Seize an Opportunity?

Rich people focus on opportunities; poor people focus on obstacles.

I live in the same reality that you live in and I understand that sometimes you feel there really are no opportunities to seize. You cannot force opportunities but you can keep your eyes open for them by learning how to:

• See the world from both your mind's eyes and your actual eyes, not one without the other.

• Not only think outside the box, but to also have no box to confine your thoughts in.

• Expand your social circle because networking is the best way to find opportunities.

Rich people vs Poor People's Minds

After reading the wonderful book, "Secrets of a Millionaire Mind" by T. Harv Eker, I defined specific distinctions between the way rich people and poor people think.

• "I create my life" – how rich people think; "life happens to me" – how poor people think.

• Rich people play the money game to win; poor people play the money game not to lose.

• Rich people are committed to being rich; poor people want to be rich.

• Rich people focus on opportunities; poor people focus on obstacles.

• Rich people focus on making, keeping, and investing; poor people focus on spending.

• Rich people admire rich people; poor people resent them.

• Rich people are bigger than their problems; poor people are smaller than theirs.

• Rich people focus on the size of themselves; poor people focus on the size of their problems.

• Rich people think both; poor people think either/or.

• Rich people live in a world of abundance; poor people live in a world of limitations.

• Rich people focus on their net worth; poor people focus on their income.

• Rich people have their money working for them; poor people work for their money.

• Rich people see every dollar as a sacred plant to grow millions; poor people see a dollar as a mere dollar.

• Rich people act in spite of fear; poor people let fear stop them.

• Rich people constantly grow and learn; poor people think they already know.

• Rich people buy luxuries last, poor people buy luxuries first.

Most importantly, thanks to the marvellous book, Rich Dad Poor Dad, the main difference between the rich, the middle-class, and the poor is this:

• The rich buy assets.

- The middle-class buy liabilities they think are assets.
- And the poor have expenses.

Coming up with solutions requires (1) a mentality that sees a positive side to every bad one, (2) patience to learn the situation from A to Z, and that requires:

Looking at the bright side – most of the time people become completely enamored in the problem and the consequences that they fail to see the true reason for the happening of that problem. Learn to look at the bright side and you will live a happier life.

Speed – never let competition slow you down; and never let competition divert your purpose to something that you would not originally do.

Efficiency – give your best to what you are doing, big or small; that's the spirit of a winner.

Good and fast decisions – sometimes people tend to be impulsive but they must not forget that they have to define the facts and opinions of an issue before coming to a conclusion. Facts are what are for certain; when there is no question about the legitimacy of the information, it is a fact. Opinions, on the other hand, are not for certain. Opinions could be said from a personal perspective. Bottom line, opinions might help you make a decision, but they will not build a constructive argument in explaining your decision. The biggest mistake you could do is to use opinions as facts in making decisions.

Strategy – is a carefully defined plan that covers both your entries and exits. Your strategy should go over and cover both your long-term and short-term goals.

Think about this:
The optimist sees the glass as half full; the pessimist sees the glass as half empty; the realist tries to figure out whether he is thirsty or not so he can drink the glass that can quench his thirst.

I could give you a speech about the benefits of being an optimist, but I would rather come up with my own word (yes, authors get to come up with their own vocabulary) and tell you to be an optirealist – which is a merge between optimism and realism where one sees the glass as half full while determining whether one wants to drink it or not.

Staying positive and optimistic is extremely important; however, it is okay if you don't reach your high expectations, so don't feel down when you don't. As the popular adage states, "aim for the moon; even if you miss, you will land among the stars." Keep on going and you will get there.

You can actually attract opportunities with your optimism and you can actually attract more problems with your pessimism when you only think of all the possible problematic outcomes that could arise.

One shortcut to finding opportunities is: **people.**

People play a major role in success and awareness to what's going on; develop friendships wherever you go, be a social person, ingrain that quality that people can't resist: **charm.**

CHARM

Some say charm is a magic spell, some say charm is an attractive feature. Truth is, charm is the ability to get a "yes" without asking a clear question. The myth that charm cannot be developed nor taught and that it is an inborn quality is, as I have mentioned, a myth.

I have dedicated a lot of time to figuring out what exactly is charm and what do people mean by charming others and what is charisma, I will summarize it all in some very important qualities:

Listening attentively when someone speaks: when you are engaged in a conversation, listen to the speaker like he or she is the only person on earth, remember that every word is important, if you find that hard to do then simply imagine the speaker a completely fascinating person; you know when people describe a charismatic quality in an individual saying "he's an amazing conversationalist"? Well, I'll make it easy for you: they mean he's an amazing listener. Being a good listener comprises many aspects, including asking questions, nodding, etc.

According to MRI scans, it's been proven that when women listen, seven parts of their brain is involved. In men, only two parts are involved, thus it's been said that women are better listeners but men can be as good, if not, better if they desired. I cannot ever overemphasize the importance of listening attentively, so make it a big deal.

Making others feel valued: the greatest gift you can give someone is the feeling of being valuable, it is the uncritical attitude of continuous positive congregation, this also includes being an amazing listener, sympathizing, simply being there, showing your concern, etc. Make people feel like they are the most fascinating individuals in the world, and they will leave your presence thinking you are.

Developing authority: authority gives you the respect of others; it gives you the respect of yourself. You can develop authority by your body language, posture, method of speaking, and method of listening. Get educated and gain general information about general topics, being an expert in a topic means controlling 29% of its conversation. Be a sophisticated and wisdomous person and people will want to listen to you. Don't speak too fast, don't speak too loudly, balance your tone of voice.

Look and dress attractively: in many cases we run across people whom we feel uncomfortable talking to because of their facial hair, or lousy breath, or messed up hair, or many other repelling features. We have also ran across people whom we felt this plea to talk to because of their intelligent look and their direct eye contact; it's very vital to keep this intelligent picture of yourself the predominant picture because that is how people will remember you physically.

Use body language for your advantage: that rhymes because we can take body language for our advantage. Keep in mind that body language conveys 55% of the message your saying, your tone of voice is responsible for 38% and what you are actually saying - your words - are responsible for a mere 7%. Think of how differently the words "I do love you" can be conveyed. It can mean "I do love you but I am busy now" or "I do love you but I hate you sometimes" or "I do love you and I always will".

Smile: whenever you smile at someone, their brain is affected biochemically and releases neurotransmitters called Endorphins, which is nature's happy drug. On the other hand, when you smile too much and laugh too much people will not take you seriously; I know that for a fact because I have known people who laugh at everything and I have realized that most people are not comfortable talking to them, including me. So the key is to laugh when something is funny, and to smile when you greet someone or when your eye meets someone else's, and remember: a genuine smile is one that lingers.

Be quick to praise people: it should be considered a crime to be in the presence of something beautiful without conveying its beauty. We can distinguish between someone who praises too much and someone who praises occasionally, but tests have shown that people are generally more interested in talking with the person who praises too much, as long as you have a charming method of praising. A charming method is ingrained when you praise specifically, be precise and be quick to praise and compliment.

Charm on Criticism:

In the psychology-oriented book, "Easy Peasey – People Skills for Life" by Allan & Barbara Pease, they clarify a wonderful way to use charm when you need to deliver criticism.

The six golden rules for a successful critique:

1-Use the Sandwich technique: praise them for something they have done, then give your criticism, then end it with another praise of something good they have done.

2-Criticize the act and not the person.

3-Admit that you also have made similar mistakes. When you admit that you have also been in their shoes, people will follow your lead because they will feel equal to you.

4-Make the criticism once

5-Never criticize someone in public.

6-End on a friendly note.

Socializing

Being aware of charm and what it takes to be developed is an excellent step in socializing, but you are also required to know other aspects of social intelligence.

Daniel Goleman divided social awareness as follows:

Primal empathy: feeling others and sensing nonverbal emotional signals.

Attunement: listening with full receptivity, attuning to a person completely.

Empathetic accuracy: understanding the other person's thoughts, feelings and intentions.

Social cognition: knowing how the social world works.

Also, he divided social facility as:

Synchrony: interacting smoothly on a nonverbal level.

Self-presentation: presenting ourselves effectively.

Influence: shaping the outcome of social interactions.

Concern: caring truly about others.

Why do people mislead problems / opportunities?

Mostly people mislead problems because they only focus on what's wrong, and when they solely focus on what is wrong they will fail to see the opportunities that are presenting itself.

There is a saying: "there are no problems, just opportunities."

Once you believe that, you will begin to see the good in the problem.

Side notes   Study body language religiously, as it is a reliable insight to how people are truly feeling. There are important signals you need to know in business and in life; for example, new research on body language reveals that motionless hands signal deceit, while rapid eye blinks show excitement; dilated pupils usually signal a persons interest in something (or someone), whilst diverting eye-contact signals a persons lack of interested and/or their inability to focus. There are many other important facts and signals that you need to be up-to-date about to apply to your daily situations with people.

Break out of your social shell, and make it a goal to meet at least one new person a day. What usually stops people from interacting with strangers is that everyone is always wondering of what other people are thinking of them; understanding that this is a common fear will ease you into talking up people. Now, the fear of strangers never subsides. We never truly grow out of our fear of strangers as children, however, our reaction to this fear shifts from crying out loud to a mere nervous feeling.

IX

CHAPTER NINE

PERSONAL MAGNETISM

"People tend to rise and fall to their level of expectations. If you reward mediocrity, mediocrity is what you will continuously get."

"Your character is plainly written on your face. Beautiful thoughts light up our facial features and vice versa."

Based on my observations, research, and multiple readings of these marvelous books:

- "Irresistible Attraction – Secrets of Personal Magnetism" by Kevin Hogan and Mary Lee Labay
- "Magnet People" by Roger Fritz
- "Advanced Course in Personal Magnetism – The Secrets of Mental Fascination" by Theron Q. Dumont

I have finally come to the conclusion on what magnetism really is and below are a few pointers of my own findings and research.

NOTE – before reading the coming pages, please keep in mind that each and every pointer below has been concluded after much effort, research, and observation. Thus, what I ask of you is to truly read every pointer like you are being handed a silver platter. Ok, speech is over. You may go on now.

- People who know themselves can count on themselves. Thus, if they trust themselves, other people will trust them too.
- Genuine people keep things simple, they do not need to impress or fool anyone.
- Magnet people radiate confidence and that puts others at ease.
- Spending an hour a day pondering your choices and current position in life is highly important to keep focus and not lose track.
- Character is defined not by what happens to you, but by what you do about what happens.

- Genius is admired; wealth is envied; power is fear; character is trusted.
- Do something that makes you different and that gives you a clear competitive advantage, both in your personal life and your professional life.
- Cultivate numerous skills and enhance them, but develop one or two skills where you can perform brilliantly.
- You are not successful until someone brags they have sat next to you in grade school.
- Usually if you are willing to be in charge, people will put you there.
- The more you need your boss, the less your boss needs you.
- Immerse yourself in the subjects that interes you and learn more about it than anyone else.
- Search for what is wrong instead of who is wrong.
- Measure your wealth by what you would have if all your money was gone.
- Appreciation is always appreciated.
- Look for ways to praise someone's character.
- Never let the desire to be liked overshadow your ability to make good decisions.
- You can never learn from your mistakes if you do not admit you have any.
- After a company reaches high and admirable places, it becomes hard to keep on innovating. The only way a company can go to the top and stay on the top is to teach experts how to listen to non-experts.
- Great people make you feel that you too can be great.
- People tend to rise and fall to their level of expectations. If you reward mediocrity, mediocrity is what you will continuously get.
- If you admire someone for their attractive qualities, add those qualities to you own personality whilst retaining your own identity.
- The secret to being naturally magnetic is to develop your love of the world. You must possess self-control and be above meanness and irritability; above resentment and malice and gossip and above all weaknesses. Develop sympathy and generosity and always be ready to give a helping hand when needed.
- The weak person loses his temper easily; the strong person controls his. Be the strong one and never lose your temper.
- If you want to be a well-liked person, you have to be a good mixer; adapt yourself to all kinds of people. Never be condescending and always be interested in people's different hobbies and interests. A great deal of diplomacy is necessary to be a people person.
- Always have an open mind; never try to convert others' thinking.
- Self-control is the predominant factor to the development of a magnetic personality.

- The quality of your voice, your use of words, your ability to put words into effective speech all disclose your education.

- Once every week, take an hour off from the world to go to a place where you will not be disturbed and rate your rate of improvement.

- Develop magnetism by demanding it.

- Your character is plainly written on your face. Beautiful thoughts have the power to light up your facial features and vice versa.

- Studying one's nature and habits will give you a passkey to influencing them. Through observing their habits, you will know their weaknesses and advantages, thus you know how to persuade them.

- Anything that will increase your confidence will increase your magnetism.

- A person with a charming personality is more attractive than a person with good looks. A charming personality can actually enhance your looks, while an unattractive personality can do the exact opposite.

- Refinement, grace and charm are weapons of personal magnetism.

- The context of your speech depends on the attitude of your speech. Thus, to be a good speaker you must cultivate both the context of your speech and your attitude of presenting it.

- You can twist around your words to make them deceitful; however, you cannot twist around your voice. Your voice always gives away your true feelings.

- Shy people think that everyone is looking at them or listening to them all the time. The cure to shyness is to understand that no matter what you are doing, other people are too busy with their own selves to be paying attention to anything else.

- We form our opinions of others based on what they say of others, and not on what they say to us. Therefore, only speak well of others, and I cannot emphasize this enough. People understand that if you speak ill of others in their presence, you will speak ill of them to others when they're no longer present.

- Cheerfulness creates power; pessimism destroys power.

- The most prized beauty is within reach to everyone.

- Human nature is trained to subconsciously rate others who are more similar to them as more attractive. Use that to your advantage in building a connection with others.

- Constantly self-educate yourself; the more you know the more you have in common with people of all personalities.

- On average, people blink 7 to 15 times per minute. When people are being deceptive, they will blink 5 to 12 times that pace.

• People subconsciously decode your level of attractiveness by the clarity of your eyes. A person with bloodshot eyes is perceived to be unhealthy, and therefore unattractive.

• In seeking out business associates, people are attracted to those who seem confident, in control, and professional.

• People are attracted to those who are similar to them. Those who share our same beliefs, cultural norms, and manners always seem more appealing.

• The left brain is more dominant in language, rational communication, and mathematics; and the right brain is more immature, emotional, and volatile. When we look to our left, we access more right brain activity than left brain.

• For right-handed people, first impressions are established when the person is seated to their right.

• Research shows that self-esteem is directly correlated to job satisfaction.

• People find it hard to be interested in those who start their conversations with "I."

• If a person feels inferior around you, they will not have any desire to be near you.

• Speaking judgmentally of others is a giveaway to others that you have issues of incompetence and insecurity. Do not play into it, and instead respond to judgmental people in a way that strengthens your position.

• People are built to subconsciously analyze two physical features to come to a conclusion on your personal hygiene, (1) your teeth and gums, (2) and the clarity of your eyes.

• Learn to look beyond what a person is saying; become sensitive to what they really need from you, whether it was more sympathy or appreciation.

• Be fully present during a conversation.

• Only give advice when someone asks for it because giving advice without being asked indicates that you undermine the person's judgment.

• Magnetic people leave others with energy because they are full of it; complainers suck the energy from others.

• People who have confidence issues will always demonstrate signs of compensation.

> These signs will radiate through the way they address others, or speak with others, or try to route the conversation back to themselves and their own interests. These signs may also include:
>
>> -Being boisterous; these people demonstrate the need to boast about things to impress people.
>>
>> -Seeking attention in everything they do, wear, or say.

-Belittling others.

-Exaggerating.

-Bullying

• Initial contact with a person will set the standard and tone for the relationship to follow. For example, if you give someone the power in the first encounter, then the same amount of submissive behavior will be expected of you in the future.

• Rarity raises your perceived value; so do not be too available.

• When you feel the need to lie about something, then there is the issue that you need to work and improve in yourself.

• A smart individual is one that learns for his/her mistakes; an even smarter individual is one that learns from the mistakes of others.

The difference between a talker and a communicator is:

• The communicator makes an effort in understanding. The talker rambles endlessly without the intention of reaching a beneficial conclusion to the conversation.

• The communicator is always seen as a giving person. The talker is always seen as a selfish and egotistical person.

How to Exude Personal Magnetism in Your Speech?

There are 3 different speeds a person speaks when communicating; fast paced, moderate paced, and slow paced.

Fast-paced speakers are generally visually oriented; medium paced speakers are usually auditory in nature; and slow paced speakers are usually more sensitive, careful, and emotional about what they say.

People who speak more quickly perceive slow communicators to be dull, boring, and slow; they often become impatient and pull out of the conversation; whereas people who speak slowly consider fast communicators to be aggressive, rude, intelligent, and quick thinkers.

What you can learn from all of these valuable pieces of information is that matching your rate and volume of speech to the person you are speaking with makes the other person subconsciously more attentive to everything you say; matching also builds rapport, and building rapport with someone is your key to influencing them and to seeming magnetic to everyone around you.

Side note   A friend of mine went through extensive speech classes to be a radio presenter, and she tells me that the she can summarize her months of extensive training in a few words: give every letter its attention and proper clear pronunciation. There, now you know the secret behind million dollar voices: speak clearly, correctly and diversify your tones according to the context of your speech.

Characteristics of magnet people:

- They are their own power source.
- They do not dwell long on their success.
- They make themselves needed.
- They get up and try again
- They never act as though the world was created for their convenience.

Instruments of magnetism:

- Making and showing the best of yourself.
- Decision.
- Preserving your energy.
- Unwavering persistence.

Chapter Ten

NEVER, EVER GIVE UP

"Our greatest weakness lies in giving up. The most certain way to succeed is always to try just one more time."
Thomas Alva Edison
"Success is going from failure to failure without a loss of enthusiasm"
John F. Kennedy

Thomas Edison is an American inventor/businessman. As his famous biographical book "Edison His Life and Inventions" by Frank Lewis Dyer explained: he is the man behind many inventions that surround and occupy our daily lives, like the light bulb and phonograph; he is even credited for the use of the word "hello" as a telephone greeting. He is the founder of General Electric and his contributions in inventions are considered one of the most significant in history. Yet, when you come to see his background you will have a hard time believing that he is the person behind these incredible accomplishments.

Thomas Edison was the youngest of seven children, three of them died before entering adulthood. He was a sick child, and because of his sickness and his dislike of the schooling systems' way of inflexible schooling and rigidity, he only had three months of schooling and continued being homeschooled by his mother who noticed Edison's curiosity from a very young age. Because of his illness, the family's financial situation was not very secure. As he recalls, "My mother was the making of me. She was so true, so sure of me; and I felt I had something to live for, someone I must not disappoint."

He began his career in New Jersey with his improved telegraph devices, but the first real step to success was the phonograph, this invention seemed magical to everyone else. He took his first job when he was 12, selling newspapers, magazines and snacks to the passengers at the Grand Trunk Railroad. Exercising his entrepreneurial skills, he set up a printing press, a chemistry lab, and a telegraph that would get information ahead of time during the civil war and he would profit by selling his papers at an inflated price.

We could say that Edison was bred into an environment that

somewhat discouraged innovation because they were yet striving to amount to their basic financial needs. Therefore, inventions and unguaranteed tries were considered a luxury the Edison's couldn't afford. However, this did not stop the curious Thomas and in 1868, he got his first patent for an invention in Boston: the electrographic vote recorder. The vote recorder allowed voters to very conveniently vote yes or no by tapping the switches, it was not popular with the congressmen of Washington but such negative feedback did not stop him.

The negative feedback he got from the vote recorder made him move to New York and dedicate his energy to the field of the telegraph, and that was when Gold and Stock Telegraphing Company gave him his first invention contracts and pursued to develop it to compete with other telegraphing firms. This gave Edison the financial freedom to focus entirely on the inventions that he dreamed of coming up with, and so he did.

Every phase in Thomas Edison's life is extremely inspirational and allow me to just stress out this important invention: the light bulb.

Mr. Edison tested over 3000 Filaments before he came up with his first version of the practical light bulb and it is said that he failed 10,000 times. Even though it was not entirely his invention, he just improved upon a fifty year old idea; other inventors had come up with similar light devices but none of these other inventions were as convenient for home and practical use. Mr. Edison retired with a net-worth of $12 million, which was a huge sum of money at the time. He passed away at October 18, 1931 (aged 84).

Let's rewind: failed 10,000 times!

Thomas Edison's thoughts on failing 10,000 times: "I didn't fail ten thousand times. I successfully eliminated, ten thousand times, materials and combinations which wouldn't work."

GUIDANCE
FROM THOMAS EDISON

- "I never perfected an invention that I did not think about in terms of the service it might give others." – Do no evil; if you promise your customers, friends, or family a specific service you have to stand by your word.
- "Time is really the only capital that any human being has, and the one thing that he can't afford to lose." – People value time less than money when time is truly the biggest asset of ours. Remember, it is only the rich who live up to the quote, "time is money."
- (1) "A good idea never was lost. Its possessor may die, but it will be re-born in the mind of another." (2) "I have more respect for the fellow with a single idea who gets there than for the fellow with a thousand ideas who does nothing." – Why leave what you can do today for tomorrow? Get off your chair and think of how good it would be if you accomplished this duty today and thereafter have nothing to worry about tomorrow. In other words, do not be a pro at procrastinating.

Just as thinking big is the first step to success, giving up is the first step to failure. Giving up is considered a crime against your own rights and here are the reasons why:
- What does success teach you? Exactly, nothing! It does come with privileges and luxuries, but does it educate you in some way? No.
- What does failure teach you? Everything. How do winners ever learn? From failing. We all failed in someway or another and maybe our first failure will be the hardest, but it is also the one that comes with the most valuable lessons.

Success has its own delicious taste and this is why we need to strive to reach it, but failure is the stairway that lifts you up to find that success. Never give up once failure meets you, rise up and embrace the challenge. We learn by failing; we learn by doing. So we have to start looking at our failures as blessings.

XI

CHAPTER ELEVEN

ONCE YOU GET THERE, GIVE BACK

"Think of giving not as a duty but as a privilege."
John D. Rockefeller Jr.

It is true that no bad deed goes unpunished, but what is even truer is no good deed goes unrewarded. I can guarantee you, the richest man in the world would not of been the richest man if he did not have a generous spirit where he thinks of the poor and the less fortunate.

The more you give, the more you will get, whether you are giving something tangible or intangible; what goes around comes back around.

Now that we put the importance of giving on the table, let me quote one of the greatest writers of all time, Kahlil Gibran, on a passage about giving:

> "There are those who give little of the much which they have – and they give it for recognition and their hidden desire makes their girds unwholesome.
>
> And there are those who have little and give it all.
>
> These are the believers in life and the bounty of life, and their coffer is never empty.
>
> There are those who give with joy, and that joy is their reward.
>
> And there are those who give with pain and that pain is their baptism.
>
> And there are those who give and know not pain in giving, nor do they seek joy, nor give with mindfulness of virtue."
>
> "It is well to give when asked, but it is better to give unasked, through understanding."
>
> The Prophet by Kahlil Gibran

After such a poetic passage, allow me to dive into the realistic psychological basis behind giving.

All human relationships, no matter how intense or superficial they are, are initiated under one self-interest basis: what will I gain from this person?

Let's not try to be monks here and claim that we do not ask ourselves that question; no matter how selfless a person may be, everyone subconsciously asks this question when starting a newfound friendship or relationship.

"What about people involved in charity work?" you may ask. Truth is, even people who are founders of charity groups find these groups for selfish reasons (most of them don't know it, yet). When someone does something selfless, they are usually getting a sense of emotional gratification in return as there is no better feeling than that of helping a person in need. Why? Because giving others provides a healing power to ourselves. Some may be more sympathetic than others, but the fact that selfless acts are selfish stands still.

Back to our point, seeing as though even selfless acts are selfish, then to appeal to people's generosity, deal with them using the indirect "I will give you such and such if you give me what I want in return" attitude. Key word: indirectly.

To keep this short, knowing this selfish nature exists in all of us, then we understand that by appealing to everyone's self-interest first in what we actually want from them is the way to get to a "yes." That is why giving is so important, and reading people smoothly and flawlessly is so important in knowing what they subconsciously want so you could consciously give it to them.

XII

CHAPTER TWELVE

Teamwork

The idea that someone can make it without an efficient team is completely unreliable.

You can be the leader, you can be the founder, you can be the creator, you can also take all the credit; but you can't do it all by yourself.

We all need encouragement, and we all need help. Surrounding yourself with people who provide these necessities and compliment what you lack is very important.

Leadership

Bones? Intestines? Organs? All people have these in common, that is enough for me to know how to treat everything that combines all these common anatomical features: with respect.

From janitor to CEO, treat people with no discrimination whatsoever and sooner or later, you will get rewarded, since what goes around comes around.

No good deed goes unrewarded.

No good deed goes unrewarded.

No good deed goes unrewarded.

I hope you memorized that.

Leadership is a wide field with numerous theories. The main qualities of great leaders are discussed below.

• Let people know how much their work means to you.

• To build credibility, you have to never put the blame on someone other than yourself. Always claim your responsibilities and be willing to own to the consequences.

• As a leader, you need to predict disastrous results and prepare accordingly.

• Surround yourself with people you admire and you will eventually become someone admired.

• Allow employees to compete with one another. Competition builds a need to excel.

• Under-promise and over-deliver.

Great leaders arouse great followers. Be a visionary who communicates his visions and goals with his fellow followers. Once you get people who believe in you enough to follow you and implement your vision, show them your belief in their vision, too. You will be surprised how far believing in people will get you.

Be compassionate; try to see everything from other people's eyes, hear from other people's ears, and try to feel every sensation from other people's bodies. Only then will you be able to truly tell someone "I know what you are saying" – and only then will you know exactly what people want and need. So what is the use of knowing what people want?

From a business point of view, understanding what people want will give you a chance to provide it for them. From a social point of view, understanding what people want will give you the asset of being socially aware of people. To go into social awareness, I will refer you to the classic book, "Social Intelligence" by Daniel Goleman.

Being socially aware means being compassionate and empathetic. Kinds of social awareness includes:

    a-Primal empathy: feeling with others and sensing nonverbal emotional signals.

    b-Attunement: listening with full receptivity and attuning to one person completely.

    c-Empathetic accuracy: understanding the other person's thoughts, feelings, and intentions.

    d-Social cognition: knowing how the social world works and functions.

Now that we know about social awareness, let us explore the areas in which a person can increase their social awareness – with social facility:

- **Synchrony:** interacting smoothly on a nonverbal level. In other words, building rapport with the person is being synchronized with the person.

> Rapport: a relationship that is harmonious in regards to how both parties (or all members of a group) relate and communicate with one another.

- **Self-presentation:** presenting oneself effectively. The way one presents oneself is always positively influenced by ones confidence. People who radiate confidence tend to always put others at ease and comfort; master the art of confidence.

- **Concern:** genuinely caring for others and being a good listener.

We are anatomically designed to miss out on useful information that might be right in front of us because of the abundant amount of information that surrounds us day and night. If we simply choose to notice such information, we will.

In an average conversation, 70% of what the speaker is saying to you simply passes from one ear to the other, playing the all-so-famous hard to get game with your brain, meaning only 30% of the words are comprehended.

"Hire the best people, but don't trust them" Donald Trump says, based on his experiences. It's a good point, you don't want to be robbed by your accountant nor do you want a traitor on your team; however, showing employees your trust in them gives them the encouragement and motivation they need to give you their absolute best, that will pay to your benefit.

So you can either hire people and trust them, or hire people and don't trust them but show them your trust (which sounds better). Use your instinct; that instant feeling you get when you meet someone new. That feeling is completely underrated because not everyone understands that our brains are trained to decode everyone's body language, tone of voice, speed of talking, facial tension or relaxation, and much else automatically. Our brains analyses all of this incoming information and classifies it – thereafter, it gives you that hunch or that gut feeling in your stomach: your instinct.

Warren Buffett, the world's best investor and the third richest person in the world as of 2011 says that he can never work efficiently with people whom he doesn't admire and feel comfortable with. Greatness inspires greatness.

No matter how gifted or rich you are, never underestimate the power of learning from your society. Seize the chance to learn, and open your eyes to the learning opportunities, even to your subordinantes.

LET'S DO THIS!
OR IN OTHER WORDS:
CONCLUSION

Fellow readers, it is within our power to shape the coming generations, and it is within our control to either drive it to prosperity or poverty.

The latter chapters discussed the techniques to accomplishing the dream and reaching the financial freedom that we all can derive.

It is a wonderful step that you chose to read this book; this shows your desire to improve yourself and your lifestyle. This also shows your potential and ambition, so I ask of you to grow that potential and ambition to imminent accomplishments.

I hope you enjoyed this book and, God willing, keep your eyes open in a couple of years for a book called

 *My* **Proven Formula of Success**

BOOKS TO THANK FOR MY MENTAL AWAKENING

1. The Definitive Book of Body Language by Alan & Barbara Pease
2. The Truth about Lying by Stan Walters
3. You Can! People Skills for Life by Alan & Barbara Pease
4. The 7 Habits of Highly Effective People by Stephen R. Covey
5. Flipping Confidential by Kriten Kent
6. Why my Horse Doesn't Listen by Vivek Mehrotra
7. Why Men Lie and Women Cry by Alan & Barbara Pease
8. The Human Odyssey by Thomas Armstrong, PH.D
9. The Inside Track to Careers in Real Estate by Stan Ross
10. Renovate to Riches by Dulworth Goodwin
11. Ordinary People, Extraordinary Wealth by Ric Edelman
12. Sound Mind Sound Body by Kirsch
13. All About Bone by Siegel
14. Irresistible Attraction – Secrets of Personal Magnetism by Kevin Hogan and Mary Lee Labay
15. Body Language by Collins need to know?
16. Small Business Start-Up Guide by Peter Switzer and Maureen Jordan
17. And Still I Rise by Maya Angelou
18. The Ten Commandments of Success by James A. Belasco
19. BRAG! – The art of Tooting your Own Horn without Blowing it by Peggy Klaus
20. Wisdom for a Young CEO by Barry
21. How to See and Read the Human Aura by Judith Collins
22. The Colour of Life by Judith Collins
23. The Art of Innovation by Tom Kelley with Jonathan Littman
24. Using Technical Analysis by Clifford Pistolese
25. Emerging Real Estate Markets by Lindahl
26. You Can Negotiate Anything by Cohen
27. Flip – How to Find, Fix and Sell Houses for Profit by Vilani Davis
28. Building Real Estate Wealth in a Changing Market by Schaub
29. The Advanced Guide to Real Estate Investing by Ken McFlory
30. The Commercial Real Estate Investor's Handbook by Fisher
31. The 5 Paths to Persuasion – The Art of Selling Your Message by Robert B. Miller and Gary A. Williams
32. Unlimited Wealth by Anthony Robbins
33. The Power of N by Meeta Lall

Made in the USA
Lexington, KY
27 January 2014